DINOS, DODOS AND OTHER DEAD THINGS

Brian Moses lives in Sussex with this wife and two daughters. He travels the UK and the Continent performing his poems in schools and libraries. He thinks that this anthology is dead good, because now that he is approaching a great age he looks back fondly at his youth, to those times when televisions were black and white and dinosaurs ruled the earth!

Yvonne Chambers and **Maxwell Dorsey** share a studio near the Arsenal ground, with Sue, and Arnie the dog.

Dinos, Dodos AND OTHER Dead Things

Poems Chosen by Brian Moses

Illustrated by Chambers and Dorsey

MACMILLAN CHILDREN'S BOOKS

First published 2003 by Macmillan Children's Books
a division of Macmillan Publishers Limited
20 New Wharf Road, London N1 9RR
Basingstoke and Oxford
www.panmacmillan.com

Associated companies throughout the world

ISBN 0 330 41564 6

3 5 7 9 8 6 4

A CIP catalogue record for this book is available from
the British Library.

Printed and bound in Great Britain by Mackays of Chatham plc, Kent

Contents

DEAD AS A DODO

They say what starts well ends well,
But for the dodo on Mauritius,
End it sadly diddid
For its start was inauspicious;
Unable to fly it was bound to die
(Did they eat it? And was it delicious?)
How sad to think it's now extinct
A no-no on Mauritius!

The flightless, defenceless dodos were killed off by 1681

Celia Warren

COLOSSAL DINOSAURS POEM

Those dinosaurs who
donned wetsuits – *they're* still having
a whale of a time.

Philip Waddell

WHY?

Why was a mammoth called a mammoth
and not an 'enormous' or a 'colossal'?
And how did they know what to call it
when they first discovered a fossil?

Brian Moses

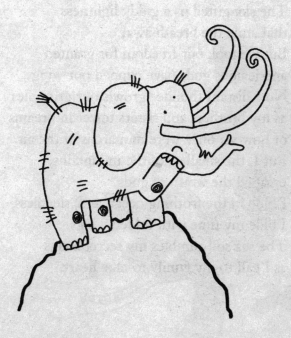

tHE LASt MountAin

Once we mountains sported wings,
soared proud above the heavens,
frolicked among fleecy clouds
and slid up and down the rainbows
that groaned with our mighty weight.
Rushing wind was our element;
we played the music of the spheres.
The sky gifted us a giddy lightness
that stole the breath away.
But we took our freedom for granted
and jealous gods have clipped our wings.
Now distant thunder growls our grumbles
as my brothers and sisters tower in dreams
of how we once were monarchs of the air.
But I, the smallest of the mountains,
escaped the wrath of gods.
I hide in the frothing ocean and, sleepless,
I bide my time with folded wings.
The sea soil rumbles my secret songs
as I call to my family to take heart.

Their trust will strengthen me
and lift me up to strike a blow for our kind,
to fly up to the sun itself if need be
to dance in our remembered freedom,
for faith, they say, moves mountains.

Mountains once had wings according to Indian myths.

Debjani Chatterjee

ENCHANTED FORESTS

Those great forests were once –
Bewitched, enchanted, filled with magic.
Now there is only
Wildlife – trees, flowers
and a row of new houses
on the edge.
Once, yes, once upon a time,
There was . . .

A roaring giant with tree-trunk legs,
A sky-high beanstalk, a golden hen,

A clearing full of wrinkled ladies
With cats, spell-mumbling round a cauldron,

A tiny cottage so pretty and quiet,
All made of sweets to tempt the children.

Also long ago a great gloomy castle
Trapped by a wall of razor-sharp thorns.

In a green misty pond a strange old frog
With enormous eyes and the voice of a prince.

A beautiful girl with laughing eyes,
Her seven friends, each a tiny man.

There was even a troll with evil hands,
A very small bridge, and a fine big goat.

All are gone now far away,
What happened I just can't say.
Perhaps it was that I just grew up,
And the magic slipped quietly away.

Les Baynton

FOSSIL

Now many years on from the Ice Age
a fossilised piece of bone
helps us make sense of the mammoth
like an ancient text message in stone.

Brian Moses

WHERE HAS DRACULA GONE?

Old Dracula was none too bright –
He was really just a sucker;
He was 'teething' still (*despite* his age!);
And his *lips* he loved to pucker!
He popped out every night, at dusk,
To get himself a bite,
And *every time* found 'something new' –
He was just a 'fly-by-night'!
But now he's vanished from the scene,
He's not been back for YEARS!
He was feeling 'peckish' when he left,
So please allay my fears:
He'd set his heart upon a *steak* . . .

Where's he got to – *any ideas* . . . ?

Trevor Harvey

SOME OTHER ARK

Two by two
the animals everybody knows
trotted, slithered,

hopped or were carried
up Noah's gangplank.
But there was some other ark

the unicorns chose:
an ill-pitched ark of bad gopher,
    an ark that leaked,

The man who sailed it couldn't
    smell or taste wind or rain
or see the Pole Star's crawl.

    He missed all olive leaves.
Drowned dragons, griffins, phoenixes
    and my precious unicorns.

Fred Sedgwick

Atlantis

Fathoms down lies old Atlantis
Beneath a turquoise sea,
A city made of marble,
Onyx, porphyry,

Houses sparkled with gemstones there,
Rubies, emeralds, jade,
Amethysts, diamonds, opals,
All in gold inlaid.

Great heroes used to swagger there,
Where now octopus and shark
Swim round its shattered columns
In the underwater dark.

Philosophers and poets there
Once quaffed a deep red wine,
Athletes rubbed on silky oils
To make their bodies shine.

Children there were happy,
They played the livelong day,
Until the dusk came sifting in
Across the sunset bay,

Until there was a rumbling,
A heaving of the ground,
And buildings started toppling
Down on the quaking ground,

And the sea came rushing at them,
And waves one mile in height,
Smashed that beautiful city,
Forever from our sight.

Matt Simpson

ROMAN INVADERS

Where did all the Romans go?
  After taking ancient Britain by storm
    They came over here in short leather skirts
    Then complained that they couldn't keep
  warm

They rubbed their bodies with stinging nettles
In an attempt to keep in the heat
But the endless drizzle and downpours of rain
Brought on their hasty retreat

They'd have known that it always rains
If they'd checked the weather report
But they jumped back into their long wooden boats
And sailed to a warmer resort.

Damian Harvey

At the Superheroes Retirement Home

At the Superheroes Retirement Home
nobody rushes to answer the phone.
It won't be a caller in distress
to interrupt their games of chess
or take them away from the television
and send them out on a dangerous mission.
The President never calls to say
'Drop everything, I need you today.'

And even the New York City Police
are doing well at keeping the peace.
Now superheroes tend to find
that dominoes occupy the mind,
but Batman likes to play roulette
while Spiderman surfs the Internet.
And no one gets out much any more
just a trip by coach to the Jersey Shore
to sit in the sun and reminisce,
how life was never as cosy as this.
The memories flutter around like birds
as the superheroes, lost for words,
look at each other and silently weep
for one more chase over the rooftops,
        one last leap . . .

Brian Moses

THERE WAS ONCE A WHOLE WORLD IN THE SCARECROW

The farmer has dismantled the old scarecrow.

He has pulled out the straw and scattered it.

The wind has blown it away.

(A mouse once lived in its straw heart.)

He has taken off the old coat.

(In the torn pocket a grasshopper lived.)

He has thrown away the old shoes.

(In the left shoe a spider sheltered.)

He has taken away the hat.

(A little sparrow once nested there.)

And now the field is empty.

The little mouse has gone.

The grasshopper has gone.

The spider has gone.

The bird has gone.

The scarecrow,

Their world,

Has gone.

It has

all

g

o

n

e

Brian Patten

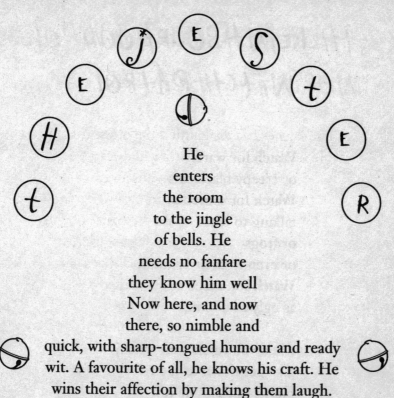

He
enters
the room
to the jingle
of bells. He
needs no fanfare
they know him well
Now here, and now
there, so nimble and
quick, with sharp-tongued humour and ready
wit. A favourite of all, he knows his craft. He
wins their affection by making them laugh.
No matter that he is of humble
birth. In royal circles
He's the king
of mirth!

Barbara Beveridge

19

NEIGHBOURHOOD
WITCH PATROL

Watch for warts
or creepy black cats
Watch for someone
talking to bats
or frogs
or even to their brooms.
Watch for a face
as ugly as doom.

when you catch your witch,
take her down to the river
Here's one simple test
You can easily give her:
      add weights to arms
      add weights to feet;
      then throw in your witch,
      where the river is fleet.

neighbourhood witch

If your warty witch floats,
then you've got one to burn.
If the witch drowns . . . Well,
let's say, that's one way to learn.

Watch for warts
or creepy black cats.
Watch for someone
talking to bats.

Mike Johnson

ALCHEMISTS

Fizz, whizz – fiery fumes!
Crackle, crunch – electrifying booms!

With bubbling pots and peculiar potions
they worked on one of the strangest notions:
turn dull base metal into glittering gold
and so have the money to buy everything that could ever
   be sold!

And just suppose they had succeeded.

It's not a secret you'd let others know
or everything, even loo seats, would have a genuine golden
glow.
No! You'd spread a story that alchemists were all old
cranks
but really they'd be the secret managers of the biggest
banks!

Tim Pointon

WHATEVER HAPPENED to inkwells

Whatever happened to | Inkwells
Ink pots
Blotters
and spots?

Whatever happened to | Quill pens
Dip pens
Fountains
with blots?

Whatever happened to | Smudges –
On noses
and fingers
and toes

Trickles of ink in the margins
Kisses of ink on our clothes.

I quite like a ball pen
or biro
A computer does everything fine
but I'd rather be back with
A quill pen

And write
in Shakespearean rhyme.

Peter Dixon

WHATEVER HAPPENED to WILL?

Where's Will with his long hair,
doublet and hose,
ink on his fingers,
ink on his nose?
Will with his parchment
and a goose feather quill,
Storytelling, play-writing
poet-actor Will.

Will's long buried,
bodily gone,
but Will's in his words
and his words live on;
words that speak
all across the years
telling of our yearnings,
tenderness and fears;
exploring love, hate,
doubt, delight;
bright with laughter
or dark as night.

Will came to London
to act on the stage,
Elizabeth's favourite,
a man of his age,
But his words are known
in many a tongue;
centuries old
and always young.

Penny Kent

tHE POWDER MONKEY

This is the moment I dread,
my eyes sting with smoke,
my ears sing with cannon fire.
I see the terror rise inside me,
coil a rope in my belly to keep it down.
I chant inside my head to freeze my nerve.

Main mast, mizzen mast, foremast,
belfry, capstan, waist.

We must keep the fire coming.
If I dodge the sparks
my cartridge will be safe,
if I learn my lessons
I can be a seaman,
if I close my eyes to eat my biscuit
I will not see the weevils.

Main mast, mizzen mast, foremast,
shock lockets, bowsprit, gripe.

Don't stop to put out that fire,
run to the hold,
we must fire at *them*
or they will fire at us.

Main mast, mizzen mast, foremast,
belfry, capstan, waist.

My mother never knew me,
but she would want to know this –
I can keep a cannon going,
I do not need her kiss.

Before 1794 children aged six upward went to
sea. After 1794 the minimum age was thirteen.

Chrissie Gittins

tHE FLiGHt oF tHE DoDo

Borne on the towering waves, they left
in a boat with billowing sails,
guided over the kraken deeps
by frolicsome great blue whales.

Their figures were round. On each stumpy tail,
the feathers were jaunty and curled
and they clacked their curving and ponderous beaks
as they fled from the eyes of the world.

On the weary days and the sleepless nights
as they forged through phosphorescence-flecked foam
croaking in chorus a heartrending song
of the land they had once called home

till they vanished forever, wing linked to wing
into the boundless blue,
to where mammoths cavort on the great purple plains
of the land they call Skangaloo,

that land outside time where the quagga plays
and rainbow stars shimmer on high,
where the dodos sit safe on their big white eggs
under a different sky.

Marian Swinger

DODOS

Where did all the dodos go?
That's something only dodos know,
But finding out's no easy task.
There are no dodos left to ask.

Rosie Kent

tHE LAMPLIGHtER

Here to the leisured side of life,
Remote from traffic, free from strife,
A cul-de-sac, a sanctuary
Where old quaint customs creep to die
And only ancient memories stir,
At evening comes the lamplighter;
With measured steps, without a sound,
He treads the unalterable round,
Soundlessly touching one by one
The waiting posts and stand to take
The faint blue bubbles in his wake;
And when the night begins to wane
He comes to take them back again,
Before the chilly dawn can blight
The delicate frail buds of light.

Seumas O'Sullivan

THE PENNY FARTHING

It's such
an amazing thing
to see. It defies all
laws of gravity. One clumsy
big wheel, the other so small.
It's a wonder that it works at all!
But the whole design just gets
madder and madder, as to climb
into the saddle you need
a ladder! But despite all
this, you must surely
admit . . .

It
would
be fun
to ride
on it!

Barbara Beveridge

34

BLACKSMITH'S LUCK

Horseshoes may be lucky, But for me the luck was bad. I made them by the hundred, That was the job I had. As tractors replace horses, The shire is disappearing. Flesh and blood evolves To metal skin and power steering

Horseshoes may be lucky,
But for me the luck was bad.
I made them by the hundred,
That was the job I had.
As tractors replace horses,
The shire is disappearing.
Flesh and blood evolves
To metal skin and power steering

Daphne Kitching

DINOSAURS

You'll have heard about us dinosaurs
In lessons when at school
Splashing in puddles
Sploshing round in pools.

Bodies big as buses
Heads pink thimble small
Tails as long as lifelines
Around your classroom walls.

We know you think we've disappeared
We know you think we've gone
And only live in pictures
Or charts with paintings on.

We've seen your illustrations
We've read the things you write
Saying that we're brainless
and only grunt or fight.

But really –

We are still around
We live on dogs and cats
Bits of bacon butty
Eels and sewer rats . . .

So careful when you wander round
And don't be fooled by lies
We dinosaurs are waiting

And you might be surprised!

Peter Dixon

tHE DiNoSAuRS JuSt VANiSHED?

The dinosaurs just vanished
Or so the story goes
But where they went and why they left
No one really knows.

I have a hunch some still remain
But live now in disguise
They're still around for all to see
If we just use our eyes.

Richard Caley

SERVANTS

They did all the housework,
washed dishes, scrubbed floors,
cleared out the grates
and answered the doors.
Once every house had one,
each family's dream,
better than vacuums
or washing machines
and the children had nurses;
life was all pleasure
for parents enjoying
both lifestyle and leisure.
Now, where are the skivvies,
the cooks and the nurses
and why does each household
ring daily with curses?

The servants are gone,
but try not to be sad
for children can call
for a mum or a dad
Who will do all the servants did.
You can live like a king
while they cook, clean and slave
and it won't cost a thing.

Marian Swinger

SQUEEZED OUT

'I squeezed clothes dry,' said the mangle.
'No question at all of that,
For once between my rollers
Things came out *very* flat.

'I lasted for years and years
And I didn't cost much to buy,
But now the tumble dryer is king
And I can't for the world think why.

'For a dryer costs lots of money
And is very expensive to run,
But mangling clothes was as free as air
And turning the handle was fun.

'Still, they stuck me out in the garden
and left me to rot away,
Until a museum curator
Caught sight of me one lucky day.

'He took me away and cleaned me
And oiled all my metal parts,
Then he put me in his museum
Of Folklore and Fine Arts.

'So now I'm a star attraction,
And I often hear people say,
"I think Great-Gran had a mangle like that.
Why on earth did she throw it away?" '

Cynthia Rider

PUFFING BILLY

Sometime-dinosaur,
rattling hulk of bones
that lumbered once
through English green,
spelt death to ancient ways
in smoke-black breath.

Now anchored
on a one-way track to nowhere,
Penny Black of steam;
collected, shown
for all to gawp and say:

He had his day,
those early engine-makers
knew their stuff.

Now silenced, still
his last breath gone:
Tyrannosaurus Bill
run out of puff.

*Puffing Billy, built in 1813, is probably the world's oldest
locomotive. It is on permanent exhibition at the
London Science Museum.*

Judith Nicholls

THE ICEBERG THAT SANK THE *TITANIC*

Well,
it wasn't
my fault, I thought
I had the ocean to myself:
drifted off the ice-shelf, was

~~~~~~~~~~~~~~~~~~~~~~~~~~

enjoying the sensation of a casual, carefree
melt. Who would have thought, in the
wide North Atlantic? Out of the mist, came
the *Titanic*! Yes, changed my life –
as I said to the wife – my big chance
to become a *celebrity*. Next
time you see a movie
with some ice in,
that'll be
me.

Mike Johnson

WHERE IS CAPTAIN HOOK?

Captain Hook has left the book; he doesn't want to play.
He shaved off his mustachio and threw his sword away.

His cannons stand deserted; his crew has got the sack.
He's put away his telescope and folded up the plank.

He waved goodbye to Wendy, said farewell to Peter Pan
and sailed a million billion miles away from Neverland.

He was tired of being a bully and a villain all the time.
What he wanted was a proper job, no more a life of
    crime.

The job centre helped Captain H. to find a new career.
where Lost Boys do not shoot at you and crocodiles are
    rare.

You have to get up early (which he doesn't really like)
but you get to wear a uniform and sometimes ride a bike.

You can see him in all weathers out delivering the mail,
a hero among postmen, known for courage without fail.

Never scared of snappy letter boxes, dogs with angry
    looks,
he puts his best arm forward and lets them chew his
    hook.

Danielle Sensier

HE USED TO BE A PIRATE

He used to be a pirate,
But now he works in a bank,
He's fine as long as no one says
Did you ever walk the . . . ?

                                        Ssh!

He'll sing a sailing shanty,
He'll talk and talk and talk,
As long as no one asks him
Did you ever walk . . . ?

                                        Ssh!

He knows of desert islands,
Has dug up buried treasure,
He'll answer any question but
Did you ever . . . ?

                                        Ssh!

He never had an eyepatch,
Though he has a parrot or two,
Talking birds that never say,
Did you . . . ?

                                        Ssh!

No one's ever asked him
But we think when he was Mid-
Shipman, many years ago, he
Did . . . ?

                             Ssh!

So what if he's an admiral?
Who cares for naval rank?
I'll shout it out for all to hear . . .
He DID walk the . . .
                        SSSSHHHH!

If he throws you overboard
You've only yourself to thank:
No one's ever lived and
said . . .

Celia Warren

LET'S ALL POGO

Whatever happened to pogo sticks
that shot you around with continuous kicks?
Nothing for years
but now it appears,
the craze has returned and they're back in the shops,
to get us all going with multiple hops.
But oh, how they've changed from a stick with a spring.
Now aerodynamic, they go with a zing!

Designed by computer.
Titanium framed
In translucent colours,
exotically named.
Adjustable height (to let Dad have a turn).
No trouble to ride them.
So easy to learn.

But use them with caution.
Take care how you go.
You'll stick in the mud if you're hopping too slow.
While out in the street,
nothing's more irritating
than getting your pogo stick stuck in a grating.

Some show-offs may demonstrate pogo pole-vaulting.
Or try triple salchows and stick somersaulting.
But while their admirers are sent into raptures,
they'll end up with multiple bruises and fractures.

So let us rejoice that the pogo's returning,
although there is something you'll quickly be learning.
Don't go pogo-sticking on Dad's bit of lawn.
He'll flip!
Then you'll wish you had never been born.

Barry Buckingham

DESPERATE PLEA

I'd really love a Hula-Hoop
and I bet, since fashion goes in circles,
one day they'll be hip again.

But in the meantime,
if anyone out there does run across one
please, *please* give me a ring!

Philip Waddell

WHATEVER HAPPENED to OLD-FASHIONED SUNDAYS?

These tedious sit on your bum days,
when decrepit great aunties would come days
and drone on about when they were young days
and you all sat up straight looking glum days,
for you had to be seen but stay dumb days,
except there were hymns to be sung days
and you knew that Old Nick got your tongue days,
if you sang saucy words to the tune.

Then suddenly Sundays were fun days,
shop in the mall with your mum days,
where scratch cards just have to be won days
and credit cards wince as they're stung days,
there are theme parks and pools to be swum days
and marathons need to be run days,
the spin has been spun over Sundays
and the week seems to be out of tune.

Maureen Haselhurst

DUNCES' CAPS

Comical, conical dunces' caps,
like witches' hats without a brim.
Unfortunate pupils, at teacher's whim,
would don such hats for appearing dim,
and stand in a corner, looking grim,
with smarting legs from a couple of slaps.

So how many yards in a mile and a half?
And when did William the Conqueror die?
Come on!
Name the capital of Paraguay.
Which ship was captained by William Bligh?
Say how many wings has a bluebottle fly,
then tell me the use of a pantograph.

What's that?
Don't know?
Come here at once!
You're ignorant, lazy, thick as can be.
Difficult questions? Fiddle-de-dee!
A teacher am I; don't argue with me.
Go stand in the corner till half past three.
And put on the CAP.
You're a no-good DUNCE!

What shame!
What grief!
What awful dread.
So cruel to the shy and the scatterbrain
who'd plead and blubber, all in vain,
immobilized by threat of the cane.
But now, no more; 'twas inhumane.
Three cheers!
The dunce's cap is DEAD.

You get two hundred lines instead.

Barry Buckingham

tHE HOBBY HORSE

The hobbyhorse lies forgotten in the attic;
The uncle who made the beautiful hobby horse is far
    away;
The boy who rode the horse, tugging the reins as the
    wild mane flowed in the wind, has grown up.
The uncle who carved the noble wooden head is far, far
    away.
The toy horse lies forsaken in the attic.

But listen!
Can you hear the distant thunder of hooves?

Gerard Benson

PiRAtE DJS

Listen out now for the pirate DJs
as they sail on the airwaves every day,
hear the rappiest, snappiest music they play
those pirate DJs.

It's the pirate DJs with their stock of treasure,
oldies but goldies to give you pleasure
this isn't work, it's a lifetime of leisure
for pirate DJs.

Just check out the deck and the sounds they blow
but they won't let you go till you've heard all the show
and they'll talk between tunes till you feel that you know
those pirate DJs.

And they're giving out all kinds of advice
from the evils of weevils to cooking with rice
and the best way to rid your body of lice
those pirate DJs.

Those pirate DJs most days feeling unwell
playing rock as they roll with the North Sea swell
they're magicians who'll have you under their spell
those pirate DJs.

And of course they're much braver than ever we think
they'd keep spinning discs if their ship should sink
till the waters roll over them, black as ink
those pirate DJs.

Then down on the seabed you'd still hear them play
rocking the rocks while the sounds ricochet,
from Amsterdam to the Bay of Biscay
those wonderful, wonderful pirate DJs.

*In the 1960s radio stations were set up illegally on ships in the
North Sea and 'pirate DJs' broadcast continuous rock music to
Britain.*

Brian Moses

PATIENCE

Whatever happened to patience?
Gran says people used to have more of it,
Dad says he hasn't got as much as he used to have,
My teacher says she's nearly run out of it
And Mum says she's run out completely.

Grown-ups tell me I should have more patience
But Mr Jones, at the corner shop, says,
'I've got no patience for cheeky boys!'
So where can I get it from?
It seems to be in such a short supply!

Coral Rumble

WHERE ARE tHE GOOD MEN

Where are they now, the cowboys
who dressed themselves in white
and rode on fine white horses
and won their every fight,

who bashed black-shirted baddies
in the good old nick of time
and married homely women
saving the West from crime,

or who rode away in the sunset
and vanished behind a hill,
lonely men riding the plains
who may be riding still?

Matt Simpson

ELVIS LIVES

Elvis lives.
He's in my class at school.
He's cool.
He walks across the playground,
swirls his hips.
He sings hymns in assembly,
curls his lip.

Elvis is alive
and well.
He took a piece of chalk
and on the blackboard
while the teacher took a walk
wrote out the lyrics of
Heartbreak Hotel.

Elvis talks.
He did not die.
He's top in Maths.
He's good at swimming, French and cookery,
good for a laugh.
He wears school uniform, school tie,
school blue suede shoes.
He keeps his head down when he's got the blues

Heartbreak hotel

or, by the bike shed,
plays an air guitar.

Love Me Tender
on the playground air.
My best friend, Elvis Presley, with his slicked-back hair.

Carol Ann Duffy

WALKING ON THE MOON

Everyone knows that men once walked on the moon.
But that was years ago.
However, it is a little-known fact
that women, also, have walked on the moon
and, unlike the men, are still walking.
It was Professor Crump (a woman)
who devised, in the early 1990s,
a method of getting to the moon
which did not involve the use of rocket fuel,
that notorious air pollutant.
She got the idea while watching *Blue Peter*,
her favourite TV programme.
It was a simple idea involving silver foil,
two empty washing-up liquid bottles, string,
a very large cardboard box, five paper hankies
and a bit of tinsel.
The first matter transportation machine
was thus invented.
Since then, many women have walked on the moon.
The logical place upon which to walk next was Mars.
Professor Crump merely added an empty cereal box
and an egg whisk and the thing was operational.
Women are, this very moment, walking on Mars.

Only last week, a whole class of schoolgirls
went there on a school trip.
Boys were not allowed.
They went on a trip to a paper clip factory near Basildon.
Professor Crump is now planning a visit to a planet
currently circling around the great star, Sirius.
She has calculated that the addition of a colander
and ten medium pastry cutters will give the machine
that necessary boost.
So, in about two weeks, women will walk beneath the
Dog Star.
Why, you ask, have the papers not been informed?
Why is even the Prime Minister completely ignorant?
Why has NASA not been told?
Who knows?
Who cares?
It is all true.
Remember to book your school trips well in advance.
Girls only.
Spacesuits provided.
Bring a packed lunch.
Well, I'm off to tea with Prof. Crump
in her cosy little dome on Mars.
Bye.

Marian Swinger

HOME FOR RETIRED DALEKS

Laser death rays
out of date:
no chance, now, to
EXTERMINATE.
Wheels squeak,
turrets creak and
slimy, greenish
fluids leak . . .

I visit them
on weekend breaks.
They say, 'Go on
for old time's sake.
We'll be so grateful,
if you do.'
'Knock, knock.'
'Who's there?'
'The Dr.'
'Dr Who?'

Mike Johnson

tHE DAYS OF OLD

Whatever happened
to the days of old? –
When kids were all
as good as gold

When every train
turned up on time
And every poem
had to rhyme

When every day
was so much fun
With lots of laughs
and endless sun

When grown-ups never said
boring things
And everyone lived like
grand old kings

When school was banned
and sweets were free
And all day long
they watched TV

When kids loved sprouts
and mustard too
And cats had puppies –
pink and blue

When the sky was green
and grass was white
And owls went off
to swim each night

When bears in caves
invented things
And yes, of course –

pigs

    had

        wings

James Carter

ONCE UPON A TIME, POETRY HAD TO RHYME

Once upon a time,
When I was at school,
The poems that we read and learnt
All had to rhyme
For that was the rule.

So children played on swings
That swung high up to the sky;
And horsemen galloped through the night
With urgent messages
From Ghent to Aix.

We read of Pobbles who had no toes;
And of Dick the Shepherd
When the winter wind blows.
We read of the Owl and the Pussy Cat who sent to sea,
And of strange aunts and uncles who came to tea.

But now –
Poems no longer have to rhyme –
Lines no longer scan
And now we can
Read of aliens stealing underpants;
Superheroes saving Planet Earth,
Whilst teachers' secret lives are revealed
For all to read.

And there's even
(For goodness sake)
A poem about a hotel run by
A friendly sssnake!

How things have changed with the passing of time!

Whatever happened to poems that scanned
And had to rhyme?

Alan Priestley

YOU LOOK SO YOUNG, DADDY, IN YOUR WEDDING PHOTO

Where's all your hair gone to, Daddy –
And what have you done with your teeth?
And why is your stomach so large
That you can't see your feet underneath . . . ?

Trevor Harvey

WHATEVER HAPPENED TO . . .

Our parrot, who squawked
Every night until dawn . . . ?
(And why have we got
A new lump in the lawn . . . ?)

Trevor Harvey

DID YOU EVER?

Did you ever . . .
Search for Narnia in your winter coats?
Look for Atlantis in your secret games?
Wait for the unicorn in a lonely playground?
Watch for a phoenix in the bonfire flames?
Hunt for a dragon in the garden shed?
Or a flying horse in the starry sky?
Or a sleeping giant? Or a talking cat?
And did you ever find them? So did I!

Clare Bevan

tHiNgS of tHe PASt

I liked being a baby a lot better,
not having to bother with words.
I remember opening my mouth
and sounds flying out like strange birds.
The comfort of talcum powder on a clean bottom.
Not having to trouble myself with zips and flushes.
Or reading. Or doing sums.
I just sat, fat, and everything was done.
I was fed by two comfy pillow breasts.
Or later, the spoon. I even got to throw
my food on the floor, smash eggs
from the fridge. Scream.

I'd never get away with all that, now
that I am eight, I've got to do things I hate
like make my own bed. When I was a baby
nobody would have thought
of asking me to make my cot.
Or dragged me along the street.
In my buggy, I put up my feet,
sucked my dummy, had a sleep.
But all that's a thing of the past.
When I'm eighteen will I be wishing
I was stuck at the top of the climbing frame?
I'll just have to accept it:
children grow up; things change.

Jackie Kay

Ye New Spell Book

Poems Chosen by Brian Moses

In *Ye New Spell Book* Brian Moses has conjured up an enchanting collection of magical verse, including a *Spell to Banish a Pimple*, a *Dragon's Curse*, love charms, old wives' tales and the following sound advice:

On Reflection

Don't practise strange spells in front of the mirror,

don't point at yourself, with a wand;

don't practise strange spells in front of the mirror,

I did – now I live in this pond.

Mike Johnson

THE TEACHER'S REVENGE

Poems chosen by Brian Moses

In an average classroom, in an average town, on an average afternoon it is not only the pupils who are staring at the clock longing for the bell to ring. The teachers are waiting too . . . An anthology of poems that reveal exactly what teachers would really, really like to do to their pupils if they could! Peek inside the staffroom and discover the secret dreams and horrible intents that lurk there – if you dare!

The Pupil Control Gadget

Science teacher Robert West
built a gadget, which, when pressed
caused consternation far and wide
by zapping pupils in mid-stride.
It froze all motion, stopped all noise,
controlled the rowdy girls and boys,
and on fast forward was great fun.
It made them get their schoolwork done,
their hands a blur, their paper smoking,
with teachers cheering, laughing, joking.
And on rewind, (that too, was nice)
you could make them do their schoolwork twice.
Robert, now a millionaire,
is selling gadgets everywhere.
Timid teachers, pupil bossed
pay cash and never mind the cost.

Marian Swinger

A selected list of titles available from Macmillan Children's Books

The prices shown below are correct at the time of going to press. However, Macmillan Publishers reserve the right to show new retail prices on covers which may differ from those previously advertised.

Title	ISBN	Price
A Nest Full of Stars	0 330 39752 4	£4.99
I Did Not Eat the Goldfish	0 330 39718 4	£3.99
The Fox on the Roundabout	0 330 48468 0	£4.99
The Very Best of Paul Cookson	0 330 48014 6	£3.99
The Very Best of David Harmer	0 330 48190 8	£3.99
The Very Best of Wes Magee	0 330 48192 4	£3.99
Don't Get Your Knickers in a Twist	0 330 39769 9	£3.99
Ye New Spell Book	0 330 39708 7	£3.99
The Colour of My Dreams	0 330 48020 0	£4.99
Are We Nearly There Yet?	0 330 39767 2	£3.99
Taking My Human for a Walk	0 330 39871 7	£3.99
The Rhyme Riot	0 330 39900 4	£3.50
The Horrible Headmonster	0 330 48489 3	£3.50
Bonkers for Conkers	0 330 41593 X	£1.95
You're Not Going Out Like That!	0 330 39846 6	£3.99
My Stepdad's an Alien	0 330 41552 2	£3.99
The Teacher's Revenge	0 330 39901 2	£3.99
Wallpapering the Cat	0 330 39903 9	£4.99
One River, Many Creeks	0 333 96114 5	£9.99

All Macmillan titles can be ordered from our website,
www.panmacmillan.com, or from your local bookshop
and are also available by post from:

Bookpost
PO Box 29, Douglas, Isle of Man IM99 1BQ

Credit cards accepted. For details:
Telephone: 01624 836000
Fax: 01624 670923
E-mail: bookshop@enterprise.net
www.bookpost.co.uk

Free postage and packing in the UK.